D0906108

FRANK SCHOONOVER

FRANK SCHOONOVER
ILLUSTRATOR OF THE NORTH AMERICAN FRONTIER

BY CORTLANDT SCHOONOVER

WATSON-GUPTILL PUBLICATIONS/NEW YORK

O
ND
237
,S4338
S 37

First published 1976 in New York by Watson-Guptill Publications,
a division of Billboard Publications, Inc.,
One Astor Plaza, New York, N.Y. 10036

All rights reserved. No part of this publication
may be reproduced or used in any form or by any means—graphic,
electronic, or mechanical, including photocopying, recording, taping,
or information storage and retrieval systems—without
written permission of the publisher.

Manufactured in Japan

Library of Congress Cataloging in Publication Data
Schoonover, Frank Earle, 1877–1972.
   Frank Schoonover, illustrator of the North
American frontier.
   Includes index.
   1. Schoonover, Frank Earle, 1877–1972.
2. Indians of North America—Pictorial works.
3. The West in art. 4. Indians of North America—
Canada, Northern—Pictorial works. 5. Canada,
Northern, in art. I. Schoonover, Cortlandt.
II. Title.
ND237.S4338S37   760′.092′4 [B]   76-16509
ISBN 0-8230-4655-9

First Printing, 1976

DABNEY LANCASTER LIBRARY
LONGWOOD COLLEGE
FARMVILLE, VIRGINIA 23901

To the memory of Frank Schoonover,
who made both life and art
increasingly beautiful compositions

78-04237

Acknowledgments

When writing a book, one acquires a legion of people to acknowledge; unfortunately, limitations of space obviate the publication of such a telephone directory. As George Moore so aptly remarked, "the difficulty in life is the choice." Certain persons, however, stand out.

Primus inter pares, Frank Herzog, master photographer and long-standing friend of Frank Schoonover; his consummate photographic skill and anecdotal treasure trove proved indispensable.

Naomi Schoonover, wife of the author, who performed prodigies in her manifold role of amanuensis, typist, indexer, and general promotatrix.

Jules Noel Wright, whose editorial and organizational assistance functioned often as the rennet in my conceptual custard.

Frank Rich, Sewell Biggs, and Josephine Hampson, who outdid themselves with their help in research and photography.

Donald Holden and Diane Hines of Watson-Guptill Publications, whose editorial excellence, patience, and personal understanding guided me surely between various Scyllae and Charybdes.

I must also thank Deedee Wigmore of Knoedler Galleries for help with research and J. Fletcher Walker for special assistance on Frank Schoonover's stained-glass windows. Thanks too to Richard Layton, artist and Schoonover student; Walter Stewart, Schoonover's secretary; and the Hon. J. Russell Eshbach, Schoonover's most distinguished model.

Unstinting cooperation was received from the Brandywine River Museum, Chadds Ford, Pennsylvania, and especially from its director, James Duff, whose personal interest and help were invaluable. Of great assistance as well was the Delaware Art Museum, Wilmington, Delaware, and its director, Charles L. Wyrick, Jr.

The University of Delaware, Newark, Delaware provided great aid in many fields of research; Drexel University Library, Philadelphia, Pennsylvania gave special corroboration of facts concerning Frank Schoonover's student activities.

I am grateful to Methuen Publications, Agincourt, Ontario, Canada for special reproductive permissions; and to the H. W. Wilson Company of New York, New York for authentication of historic correspondence.

To anyone who feels himself herein slighted by omission, my profound apologies; omniscience and perfection were never numbered among my vices.

CONTENTS

COLOR PLATES

PREFACE

The period from 1880 to 1920 is often called The Golden Age of American Illustration. At a time when illustrators had an enormous and enthusiastic public, there were many candidates for the title of "America's most popular illustrator." Although it is noo my intention to enter my father's name in this popularity contest, Frank Schoonover was certainly one of the leading "Contenders." Virtually ignoring popularity—which came by itself—Frank Schoonover produced a vast flow of book illustrations, magazine illustrations, and commissioned and noncommissioned paintings.

Most of his paintings are still in collections in the Brandywine region of Pennsylvania and Delaware where he studied, lived, and worked among the prodigious concentration of talented artists created by Howard Pyle, whose inspired teaching produced several generations of notable illustrators.

In this book I hope to show Frank Schoonover's mastery of action, which underlay his lifelong conviction that "the picture must tell a strong and memorable story." I also hope to bring out something of my father's intriguing personality. As his friend Kenyon Cox said, "You cannot have the art without the man, and when you have the man you have the art."

It is extremely difficult to avoid being trite in trying to get across the fact that some artists can portray people better than others. Schoonover had a deep interest in people of all ages, particularly children, and this trait enabled him to relate to the magazine or book reader on a very intimate level.

The task of revealing Frank Schoonover is made easier by the fact that he left behind so many documents that reveal himself. Schoonover not only kept a diary for over 40 years but maintained day books for his entire career, starting with a record of his first published picture. The detail and completeness are awesome. He meticulously recorded each drawing or painting: number; publisher, author, and title of story or book; medium and painting surface (kind of canvas, if canvas); year, day, rate, and amount of time spent working; name of mobel, time employed, and pay; date of completion and shipping information; plus any miscellaneous details. Sometimes, like a diary, pages would record visitors and their names, sales (price in a secret code), notes on trips (especially fishing), family notes, and reminders. In addition, there are files and files of personal papers and photographs of all sorts.

I guess "budget of memories" was his favorite phrase during the latter part of his long career. In the late 1950s and 1960s when I was trying to catch him on tape on Wednesday nights in the studio, he would putter around (always turning up something new) until, finally comfortable in his favorite rocking chair that Howard Pyle had given him, he would say, "Well, I guess there's no escape now. Are you ready to get on with my budget of memories?"

There is obviously too much to work with. Out of this wealth of material and my intimate association with the artist as his only son, I have tried to reproduce those words and pictures that portray the artist and the man.

In an interview with Anthony Higgins, Associate Editor of the *Evening Journal* in Wilmington, Delaware, on October 5, 1962, the artist stated: "I used to use a dark palette, lately I find my colors are getting brighter." Higgins writes: "That is the way we look at Frank Schoonover. He and his colors keep getting brighter. They will keep on getting brighter for generations of gazers long after he has painted his last picture in the land he loves."

The author hopes that the reader catches this spirit.

A page from Schoonover's day book, 1911, pen and ink on paper, 8" x 10". Courtesy Private Collection.

Paxton Portrait of F.E.S., *oil on canvas, 20" x 16". Painted 1921 by William Paxton of Boston, Massachusetts. Courtesy Private Collection.*

INTRODUCTION

Frank Schoonover was, above all, an artist of action. From his first commercial drawing in 1899—*The Cow,* a chart showing the correct cuts of meat—to his last painting in 1968 —*The Spirit of the Windigo*—more than 4,000 pictures later, his work was infused with vitality and drama. Particularly dramatic were his compositions of Indians, cowboys, and other forceful characters of the American and Canadian West, which provided illustrations for many successful books. For models he chose persons of strong physique and character. "I never painted a weakling," proclaimed Schoonover.

Endowed with fantastic curiosity and a photographic memory, Schoonover dedicated his life to the outdoors. He was an adventurous traveler, enthusiastic canoeist, and famed fisherman who was able to recreate the outdoors in paint or in words for he often illustrated his own writings.

The Golden Age of Illustration

Frank Schoonover lived and worked during the Golden Age of Illustration, which burgeoned in the last half of the 19th century and flourished through the 1920s. Changes in social structure and printing technology gave impetus to a new blend of literature and illustration—realism, romance, adventure, and entertainment. Color was the keynote. The writer and illustrator worked in collaboration to create an environment in pictures and words through both powerful portraits and action scenes, and through the spirit of magic, enchantment, adventure, and romance in prose. Thus the illustrator-painter came into being.

The painter as illustrator can be said to be a Renaissance concept. One has merely to think of Giotto's frescoes in the Scrovegni Chapel in Padua or any of the myriad historical, mythological, and religious canvases produced from the 14th to the 18th centuries to see that the primary concerns of the artist were style, technique, and composition. To a certain extent it can be said that the subject matter per se was secondary. The painting itself served as both text and illustration.

The origin of the illustrator as painter must be found in the illuminators of the medieval manuscripts where the text provided the basis for the artwork. This tradition reappears strongly in the 19th century when vast improvements in printing processes gave rise to art as reportage. One result of this innovation was the creation of a new kind of artist: the illustrator whose work appeared in print, as distinct from the easel painter who exhibited at the salon.

Howard Pyle

On the American scene, Howard Pyle exemplified the illustrator-painter. He thought of the book as a total enterprise. Binding, type, and layout were as important as the text and illustrations. His production of *Robin Hood* in 1883 heralded a new style in book design. His technical skill, creative imagination, and dramatic power elevated the status of illustration to great heights. His 100 students at Drexel Institute in Philadelphia, in his summer classes at Chadds Ford, Pennsylvania, and in his school in Wilmington, Delaware, were inspired by Pyle as a writer, artist, and teacher. All responded to his high standards of workmanship and his indelible influence.

The students of Howard Pyle may be referred to as the second generation of illustrator-painters. Among them were Stanley Arthurs, Clifford Ashley, Harvey Dunn, Gayle Hoskins, N. C. Wyeth, and of course Frank Schoonover. Each artist is remembered for his own special characters and settings. Schoonover chose the Canadian wilderness and the great open spaces of the American West, the rugged faces and figures of cowboys and Indians, for his dramatic compositions. He also holds the spotlight as the Pyle student with the longest painting career: he lived 95 years, from 1877 to 1972.

Schoonover Tells His Story

Frank Schoonover had his own lively writing style, as revealed in this autobiographical account written for Muriel Fuller, the editor of *More Junior Authors*, published by the H. W. Wilson Company, when she requested information for the Schoonover entry. The letter was dated April 14, 1958, and written from the artist's studio in Wilmington, Delaware.

My dear Miss Fuller:

Here is something about the why of my art beginning. I was born August 19, 1877 in a little village called Oxford in New Jersey. This was a mining town and iron ore was the product. My father had oversight of the small industry and the blast furnace. Was that something to remember! Eventually the family settled in Trenton, New Jersey, about two blocks from the Delaware River. I had a boat and some minnow nets and traps. I caught minnows and kept them alive for sale to bass fishermen. This was a first business venture. Part of each summer was spent with my grandmother, who lived in Bushkill, Pike County, Pennsylvania. I was supposed to help her because she lived alone. I don't believe I was of much help because I spent most all of the time along the Bushkill streams looking for things. Just little fish and that sort of thing. I built little raceways along the bank and I had a whole lot of water wheels going. On some I had spools and a lot of thread and I could take this thread down the stream and tie a little boat on the string, start the water wheel and pull it up the stream. I also built a flat bottomed boat that leaked a lot.

Well, my grandmother wondered about all this and kept asking what I was going to do when I grew up. That was quite a question. I told her I was not quite sure but I would do something that would have to do with the streams and trees. I really thought I would be a builder of bridges. Just little bridges for one horse and wagon. Of course I know now that this was the beginning of my making pictures of bridges and streams. I made pen and ink drawings. I did pretty well with houses, barns and little buildings. As I look at one of these now I realize that my father gave me a real bit of help with the perspective business. It was quite wonderful. The vanishing point was an established affair after we rigged up a pencil and notches and string. One end of the string was held in my mouth so that there was always the same distance from pencil to eye. A building could be two spaces high and a tree four or five. It really worked out and I did well, as I say, with buildings. They were like blocks and that's the way I thought about them. I could not manage trees at all. Did

Frank Schoonover's birthplace
in Oxford, New Jersey,
photographed by the artist in 1953.
Courtesy Private Collection.

Frank E. Schoonover at age 10, 1887.
Courtesy Private Collection.

A Lesson in Perspective, *pen and ink on board, 11" x 8".*
Drawn by the artist in 1898. Courtesy Private Collection.

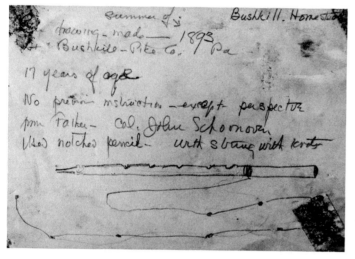

Back view of **A Lesson in Perspective.**

not know what to do with masses. Downtown in Trenton I got some oil colors and started to paint. The first bit was a still life. Apples in a splint box. It's still about. Then as I said there was a boat in the river. There was a home-made easel rigged up in the back of the boat. I went into any little cove where no one could see me. I didn't want anyone around. There were several paintings made. Landscapes, I called them. Evenings now and then I kept on with the pen and inks. I copied Howard Pyle drawings, all I could find.

I went to a preparatory school in Trenton. My parents had an idea that I ought to go to Princeton eventually and study to be a minister. That would be in the nature of eight years or more. Well, I tried the entrance examinations, but I lacked Greek. So I studied all summer with a minister and made out fairly well with it, even getting into the writings of Matthew, Mark, Luke and John in the original. But mind you there was still that picture of making pictures of streams and bridges and trees. So I spent a lot of time on the river—the Delaware—in my boat looking around in the little inlets and making sketches by day and copies of Howard Pyle pen and inks at night.

Well, I finished the school in Trenton. That was in 1896. Bushkill again in the summer. Thinking about the fall and college and I did not seem to be very happy about it; I returned to Trenton and in a copy of the *Philadelphia Inquirer*, a September issue, I read all about the offerings of Drexel Institute. There in Philadelphia at 32nd and Chestnut, it said that anyone with a desire for illustration could have the instruction in that kind of art under the tutelage of Howard Pyle. That if the work in hand would pass the judgment of (great master to me) Howard Pyle. Well (and you can understand how this seemed to be an answer to it all) that was it. The main requirement to enter his lecture classes—Monday, Friday afternoons, and Saturday morning—was the product of imagination. Could you think of and make up a drawing of your own idea—in charcoal? At home in Trenton, I had been making a lot of pictures in just that way. The subjects were all incidents—so I called them—but later there was something added by Howard Pyle —these ideas were to be thought of as facts. They were certainly facts to me. I had drawings of facts that were a part of my life. Catching minnows with a net, bringing home a Christmas tree—that was a good one—so I was told later by H. P. because I had showed a covered bridge with its black opening and an owl in the tree. That was good because it was very late in the day—snow on the ground—and the boy seemed to be afraid of the bridge and the owl. There were others—fishing through the ice, streams, little bridges, and a boy looking under a stone for nothing much. Mr. Pyle looked over them all and said because of the creative thought he would admit me into the classes. I came into the group the day before Christmas 1896.

I was fortunate to win two summer scholarships at Chadds Ford. The second summer at Chadds Ford I illustrated two books secured for me by H. P. One *A Jersey Boy in the Revolution* and *In the Hands of the Red Coats*. Other books followed: a long serial for *Collier's, Cardigan,* by Robert W. Chambers, then a set of illustrations for *McClure's Magazine.* For *The Lane That Had No Turning* by Sir Gilbert Parker, I went to Quebec and Cap Rouge for the commission. I lived at Cap Rouge and made a great many sketches in colored crayons. Sir Gilbert Parker greatly approved of all of this. I must have made some fifty small and large pictures for his book.

After this I went to Scranton, Pennsylvania at the time the first great coal strike occurred. I lived in the home of one of the workers. Many drawings were made on the spot for the story called *Children of the Coal Shadows.*

Next came work for Scribner's in 1903, *In the Open*, by Mary Raymond Shipman

Female Portrait, *oil on canvas, 29" x 14 3/4", 1899.*
Courtesy of Sewell G. Biggs Private Collection.

Andrews. Also I made a big poster to advertise this. Another book from Scribner's, *The Blood Lilies* by Fraser gave me seven full pages of illustration.

The Deliverance, by Ellen Glasgow of Richmond was a real assignment. I travelled through the tobacco fields with the owners, and worked with Miss Glasgow on the illustrative layout.

Now comes the trip to Canada and the two stories (my own) published in *Scribner's* magazine in 1905—*The Edge of Wilderness* and the *Winter Harvesters*. Then followed a grand lot of stories by Lawrence Mott, which were located in the same part of Canada that I had covered in the winter dog-team trip producing my own stories. So you see it all fitted in and it was a wonderful lot of pictures—so I was told—I didn't say that. For Mott's story, *Jules of the Great Heart*, I prepared a portrait-sketch of the great half-breed hero to show to the writer and his mother and it was approved because it looked like her son who had written the serial. Was that something, what business!

Outing Magazine came into the picture now. Casper Whitney was the editor. I wrote and illustrated a whole handful of things for him: *The Pool, The Forest, The White Birch*—woods, streams, bridges again. It all goes back to the early days in Bushkill when my grandmother wanted to know just what I was going to do with myself.

Now I see here by my book in 1906 I went to Denver, Colorado to get the story of Judge Ben B. Lindsay and his youth court. Next to Butte, Montana for the very long serial of Montana and the fight for the Minnie Healy, a copper mine. Anaconda has just published a little book about this. But I was way out ahead.

Now Henry Van Dyke of Princeton (I really did get to Princeton, you see after all) comes into the studio with his *Holiday in a Vacation*. Here was another series for Scribner's. And I guess Henry, that is Van Dyke, was no end pleased because I put his daughter in the canoe—made the picture look like her—Brook Van Dyke was her name.

A grand time followed with more Van Dyke for *Outing Magazine*. Also the company of Jack London entered. Quite a pair—the two. There were many interesting associations and action-packed stories to illustrate for some of the writers that everybody remembers! Edgar Rice Burroughs, Zane Grey, Elsie Singmaster, Thomas Janvier, Rex Beach, and many more. Every once in a while someone tells me how Beach says I made him. Imagine! You see I chose to work on the first story he ever had accepted. This all came about because the publisher sent me two stories to Wilmington for me to make a choice for pictures—both were Canadian and had a Christmas idea. I chose the one by Beach.

Early in 1910 I went up to Scranton, Pennsylvania, for *Harper's* and did a story and made the drawings about the women and girls who were working in the silk mills. I got into a bit of trouble because I put young faces in all the pictures. It was printed anyway.

Following that there was a period of helping with the murals in the Hudson County Court House. That was in Jersey City, New Jersey. How well I remember painting the Indians who had paddled out to sniff at the Half Moon. Hudson's ship, you know.

My own story and illustrations for *In the Haunts of Jean LaFitte* came out in the December 1911 issue of *Harper's*. I lived on location way down there on the Bay of Barataria—where Jean and his fellows had their haunts—the main one. Now there is an interesting item here. While I was down there (there meaning New Orleans) my very helping wife went to the library to gather all the material in hand about LaFitte. And who do you suppose came in for the same material? None other than

Rex Beach. Rex gave up the idea to write about LaFitte when he was told that Mrs. Schoonover had all the books over there at the far table, all the stories and facts about the pirate.

Houghton Mifflin decided that I should illustrate *Evangeline*. This was a real challenge—but I knew the country. I had traveled there and I knew the people. I had only to visualize the people in the steerage of the ships coming to the New World, and to express their emotion for it revealing spiritual beauty.

I could ramble on, but this gives you some idea about me. All I have written and drawn goes back to the early days in Bushkill when my grandmother wanted to know just what I was going to do with myself. Woods, streams, bridges, nature, the wilderness—they are all in my work; and the people I painted are rugged as their environment.

This is all interesting—to me at least.

Frank E. Schoonover

Pyle's Classes

In 1895, Howard Pyle and the Drexel Institute trustees devised a plan to stimulate interest in the art department by offering prizes and scholarships, the first scholarship to honor Francis I. Drexel, founder of the Institute. Duncan MacAlister, then President, perceived that Pyle was the right man to institute a course in illustration. Although the fundamentals were well taught at Drexel and at the Pennsylvania Academy of Fine Arts, also in Philadelphia, most students were fitted only to make exhibition pictures; no matter how good they were, they were seldom sold. But publishers were becoming interested in illustration. There was a demand for story pictures in books and magazines. The illustrator-painter was in the spotlight.

Years later, Schoonover talked about the training of an illustrator. "Technical training is necessary, but it must be subordinated to the training of the imagination. . . . Good illustrations are storied pictures, and they tell some phases of the story better than do words. They must convey the same thought and action as do the stories. They must be convincing, fitting in detail, embodying the same power of imagination, the same humor, romance, and action. Howard Pyle taught us this."

Schoonover won a Drexel scholarship: "To hear on the day before Christmas that I had been admitted into Howard Pyle's class on Composition was my greatest Christmas present, as I felt I was on my way to some kind of a living. I couldn't see that art offered any security at the time, other than illustration. I don't know, but it's pretty much the truth today. I felt very honored because his class was a pretty strong one—made up of big shots! Clyde O. Deland, Jessie Wilcox Smith, Maxfield Parrish, Thornton and Violet Oakley, and others.

"So I started to work on making compositions. Of course, I was bewildered as to what to do, so I thought the only thing was to make pictures of things I knew. I was living in the country, and I remember clearly three pictures I made: one was a farm scene in the fall—a field of corn. Huskers were hand-husking the ears and throwing them into the bottom of a wagon, which was drawn through the rows. Another was of some boys in a little stream with poles and some mosquito netting fastened to the poles catching minnows for bait. The third showed a boy carrying a Christmas tree toward a covered bridge. Mr. Pyle was strangely impressed, no doubt noticing signs of his type of work. As I said, I had been copying him for years, no reference was made either way here! Yes, Mr. Pyle was impressed, 'You have learned the secret of creativity. Work hard, don't be discouraged ever, and make this year a flying start. We'll see how you make out soon enough.' "

Schoonover's career did not make a flying start in Mr. Pyle's very demanding class.

Stanley Arthurs, Howard Pyle, and Frank Schoonover in Mr. Pyle's yard, circa 1903. Courtesy Private Collection.

Stanley Arthurs, Howard Pyle, and Frank Schoonover in Mr. Pyle's Franklin Street Studio, Wilmington, Delaware, circa 1903. Courtesy Private Collection.

Portrait of the artist at age 20, 1915. Courtesy Private Collection.

"I ya longtemps que je t'aime. Jamais je ne t'oublierai," *pen and ink on board, 8" x 10". From* The Lane That Had No Turning *by Sir Gilbert Parker, Doubleday, Page & Co., 1902. Courtesy Private Collection.*

His happiness over his good fortune to be there was boundless indeed, but the big, domineering man started new students at the back of the classroom. This in itself was not enough; it was his custom to select each week only ten compositions for criticism. Month after month went by and Schoonover's creations rarely made the weekly Friday afternoon criticism agenda. He was beginning to understand Mr. Pyle's warning about discouragement. During this trying period, however, he had found a strong ally. Seated next to him was Stanley Arthurs, later to become a noted painter of historical subjects. His work had achieved the critique session. Stanley Arthurs and Frank Schoonover became lifelong friends. They took over the chores as class monitors, and as their talents developed the great teacher felt a fatherly concern for them. They were his favorites— helpers and friends until the end of his days.

According to the Drexel University News, the legend runs that Schoonover received his first paid assignment while at the Institute. The drawing of a cow showing cuts of meat was needed in the Department of Domestic Science. For many years his carto-graphical idyll was hung and used there. A recent issue of *Drexel University News* features an article on "Drexel in the 90s," and *The Cow* is pictured on the page captioned: "The cow, to the left of the clock, was drawn by Frank Schoonover, a Drexel student, who later became a well-known illustrator. The drawing brought Schoonover his first pay check."

Schoonover had won scholarships to Mr. Pyle's exclusive summer school in Chadds Ford, Pennsylvania in both 1898 and 1899. These July and August sessions were in actuality the beginnings of what is now known as "the Brandywine School." Member-ship, especially by scholarship, was highly prestigious.

Among Schoonover's now well-known colleagues in the Brandywine School were Stanley Arthurs, Clifford Ashley, Gertrude Brinckle, Ethel Penniwell Brown, Clyde DeLand, Harvey Dunn, Anton Fisher, Philip Goodwin, Elizabeth Shippen Green, Gayle Hoskins, W. H. D. Koerner, Charles MacLellan, Anne Moore, Thornton Oakley, Violet Oakley, Maxfield Parrish, Henry Peck, Katharine Pyle, Olive Rush, Jessie Wilcox Smith, Henry Soulen, Henryette Stadelman, N. C. Wyeth. Then it was not long before Pyle was passing on to Schoonover work that rapidly established him with the greats in the publishing world.

Howard Pyle was obsessed with authenticity. Pyle encouraged his students to paint from real objects, to visit the locale. Schoonover once paid a New York City costumer $40 just to find out the correct number of large buttons on General Lafayette's dress uniform coat. He spent precious hours in libraries gathering facts to lend authenticity to his work.

Pyle taught that imagination is the key to reality and Schoonover learned that lesson well. During 1918 and 1919 Schoonover, working entirely in the United States and never seeing the war firsthand, produced a series of 15 full-page World War I action pictures—one each month—for the *Ladies' Home Journal*. Each scene was so timely and so realistic that the War Department could not believe he had not taken part in the action he portrayed. His canvases startled the viewer with their realistic storytelling beyond photography. They bore an uncanny quality of instant replay. The pictures now belong to the Department of Defense.

The Canadian Northwest

"Today is August 19th, my 25th birthday," Schoonover told Pyle. "I just don't feel right about the work I am doing now for I am having to project to the public too much that is really not out of my experience. You have given me the skill. To progress the way you say you can have faith that I can, I feel that I must pick a field in which I can develop a relationship with the public that will say, 'This rings true; he knows because he has been there.'"

In the picture above The Cow Poster *stands on the sideboard, poster paint on board, 36" x 24". Used as a poster in Home Economics Department at Drexel University in 1898. Photo published in Drexel University News, August 1975. Courtesy of Drexel University Library.*

Doorway to Howard Pyle's Studio in Chadds Ford, Pa. in 1898. Schoonover stands at the extreme left posing as a model for fellow students. Courtesy Private Collection.

A winter camp photographed by Schoonover in 1904 on the Canadian expedition in Quebec about 50 miles north of Cape Rouge. From American Boy Magazine, "Bringing the Outdoors In" by Frank E. Schoonover, March 1921. Courtesy Private Collection.

F.E.S. in front of his tent at the northernmost part of the Hudson's Bay Expedition, 1904. From The Edge of Wilderness: A Portrait of the Canadian North *by Frank E. Schoonover, edited by Cortlandt Schoonover, Methuen Publications, 1974. Courtesy Private Collection.*

"Where have you in mind?"

"The Canadian North country, the Indians, the Eskimos, the great unknown country up there."

"Go," said Mr. Pyle.

Upon his return from spending the long winter of 1903 in northern Quebec and Ontario, crossing Hudson Bay by dogsled with two Indian guides, living with the Indians, and experiencing first hand just as much as he possibly could, he returned armed with a treasure of sketches; crayon, pencil, and charcoal drawings (it was too cold to use oil paints); photographs and notebooks; and above all a deep understanding and knowledge of the people and the vast country.

Schoonover put his newly acquired powers to work at once and quickly found that in the short period of a year he had made of himself a unique producer of a product that was in great demand from a number of publishers, particularly magazines.

The first story and drawings to come out of his Canadian experience appeared in the April, 1905, issue of *Scribner's* magazine. It bore the intriguing title "The Edge of the Wilderness" and was the artist's account of his daring travel in the bitter Canadian winter far from civilization. Illustrated with nine colored drawings in pastel, this story was part of a two-part serial. The second part, entitled "Breaking Trail," appeared in *Scribner's* May, 1905, issue. These two issues not only established Schoonover's reputation as a man who had "been there" but as an artist who was exhibiting strongly to the public his potentialities as a writer and illustrator combined. But much more than that, they demonstrated his passion for accuracy, his fascination with and awareness of significant detail, his ingenuity, persistent concern with dramatic action, and above all his imagination—what Pyle called "mental projection."

Hopalong Cassidy

In 1905, Clarence Edward Mulford, well-known writer of Western stories, conceived of a character whose combination of charisma and quirks was to canonize him in the annals of cowboys and Indians. The character was a Tom Mix type shoot-'em-up wrangler, except for the fact that he had one leg shorter than the other. His name was Hopalong Cassidy (see the color plate on page 49).

Mulford's idea was good enough, but he wasn't sure that his character would come across creditably in print. It so happened that his friend Schoonover was about to embark on an assignment for *McClure's* magazine in Denver, Colorado. He conned Schoonover into keeping a watchful eye out for stump-legged cowboys.

Schoonover had been given two assignments on this trip. One was to illustrate an article by Lincoln Steffens dealing with the work of Judge Ben B. Lindsay, an innovator in the field of justice for juveniles. The other was to research the copper mining business in Butte, Montana, for a story by C. P. Connolly, "The Fight of the Copper Kings," which *McClure's* planned to publish in their May, 1907, issue. Schoonover went west, armed with sketch pad, canvases, chalks and paints, and the omnipresent, indispensable camera. The photographs he took were fodder for many subsequent years of Western illustrations.

After completing his assignment in Denver, Schoonover headed north to the Anaconda Mines which bore the enchanting name of Minnie Healy. While there, one day he saw a short-legged cowboy sitting awkwardly on a corral fence. Remembering Mulford's commission, he drew several sketches of this as-yet-hypothetical character. The model's name is unknown; Schoonover did however purchase his boots (which still exist). Whoever this nameless and shoeless person was, the character he portrays went on through novels, pulps, comic books, films, and TV serials to become a household word.

While at the mine, Schoonover also made the acquaintance of Rex Randerson, a local

Indian on horse in
Blackfoot Reservation.

Cabin in Montana.

Street scene in Montana.

Cowhands in Montana.

Street scene in Montana.

The artist watching
preparations for the Sun Dance
of the Black Foot
Indians, 1906.

F.E.S. on Patches, outside Butte, Montana, 1906.
Courtesy Private Collection.

Cowhand in Montana.

Butte, Montana.

27

sheriff, who owned a picturesque though bony horse. Keith Prickett used this character in a story based largely on Schoonover's observations, and the horse went on to fame in a poster for the Colt Firearms Company (see the color plates on page 109). He also inspired the poster *Tex and Patches* (see page 52).

Europe

In 1907 Schoonover made an extended trip through the art world of Europe. In the company of a wealthy Wilmington friend, Richard Sellers, whose father, William, was a founder-director of the Philadelphia Academy of Art, he made the grand tour in style. On arrival at LeHavre, Richard's mother joined the two and accompanied them after Richard had bought a big Fiat touring car and hired a chauffeur.

The European trip was undoubtedly the most valuable expedition of Schoonover's life, although the trips to the West and to Canada have been better documented and publicized. The Sellers spared no expense or effort to see that Schoonover was presented with the best art in Europe, and they indulged his love of the outdoors by putting the big Fiat practically at his command in the Alps. The artist claims to have gotten the most pleasure from the climbing and the most artistic stimulation from Rome, where the time spent in concentrated study later provided great assistance in painting such pictures as *Pope Benedict XV Greeting President Wilson*, one of the series of 15 war pictures which were single-page features in monthly issues of the *Ladies' Home Journal* in 1919.

Back to America

Sellers brought the car back to the States where it figured in a freak accident one Sunday afternoon as the two friends were taking a drive along the Wissahickon Creek in Philadelphia. On entering the stone bridge tunnel just a few miles into Fairmount Park on Wissahickon Drive, Sellers swerved to avoid hitting another car. In doing so he was thrown clear, but the car turned over and crushed Schoonover's left elbow. In the hospital the arm was saved, but the surgeon asked the artist to tell him in what position he wanted the joint set because the doctors did not believe he would ever be able to move it again.

"Well, that's the arm I use to hold my palette, so let's set it just right so I can do that."

"We'd have to use the palette as part of the cast. You're asking the impossible," said one of the doctors.

Sellers, unfamiliar with the impossible, rounded up a palette in jig time and the weird cast was made. Not only was it successful, but they rigged it with a cranking device of ingenious design that enabled Schoonover to gradually regain full use of the joint! Once healed, the injury was never noticeable. While the arm was in the strange cast, the artist allowed himself the loss of just one week of work. Mr. Pyle fixed him a special table of which he became very fond and which proved much better than the palette he had been using. Each evening Schoonover lovingly cleaned the working area.

Hudson County Courthouse

In the spring of 1910 Howard Pyle received a commission for three large murals for the Renaissance-style Hudson County Courthouse then nearing completion in Jersey City, New Jersey. In charge of the decoration of the building was Francis D. Millet, an old friend of Pyle's, hence the choice of Pyle for the murals in the Freeholders' Room, the most important room in the building. This was the most extensive undertaking in Pyle's career; he had to engage Frank Schoonover and Stanley Arthurs as assistants to transfer his full-size cartoons to canvas, and later, as the deadline for completion approached, to paint most of the background and some of the figures. Notwithstanding the combined efforts of this troika of illustrators, Schoonover's records show that work was not completed until October 13, 1910—a full 23 days after the official opening of the courthouse!

Peter Stuyvesant and the English Fleet, *right side of mural in Hudson County Courthouse, Jersey City, New Jersey, 1910. Reprinted by permission of the County of Hudson of the State of New Jersey by Edward Clark, County Executive.*

Schoonover working on the mural.

Life in an Old Dutch Town, *mural for Hudson County Courthouse, unfinished, 1910. Reprinted by permission of the County of Hudson of the State of New Jersey by Edward Clark, County Executive.*

Hendryk Hudson and the Half Moon, *study on easel in Pyle's studio, July 1910.*

The largest of the three murals, measuring 9 feet by 36 feet, depicted *Life in an Old Dutch Town*. By June 9 the canvas was stretched, and the transferral of cartoons went on until the 19th. Schoonover spent the rest of the month painting the foreground, the sky, and the water. (During this time he was dividing his interest between the mural in the Rodney Street studio and his first fianceé in Philadelphia.)

The second mural, *Hendryk Hudson and the Half Moon*, was begun after the Fourth of July holiday. As the large canvas was still not complete and Schoonover was assigned to paint the Indians and canoes in the second canvas, Philadelphia took a definite back seat for the month—indeed, for the next three months. His daybook records everyone's disgruntlement. On July 28, "Mr. Pyle retired—did not care very much for our efforts." Schoonover went off to Trenton, but not without making the unusual notation in his records: "July 29—Mr. Pyle working."

Peace returned to Rodney Street with the arrival of August. By the middle of the month Pyle, Arthurs, and Schoonover were having dinner at the Jersey City train station prior to work *in situ* at the courthouse. The third mural, *Peter Stuyvesant and the English Fleet*, occupied the month of September. Schoonover again worked on sky, water, and some of the figures. On the big canvas he painted the houses, the apple trees, the sea captain's head, and some merchants; on the smaller mural he executed one of the ships.

The canvases were packed off to Jersey City and put in place in the courthouse between September 30 and October 13. This left Schoonover free to begin illustrations for Rex Beach's "Captain Innocencio" for *McClure's* magazine and to return to Philadelphia for the selection of "wedding garments and a bedstead."

Although Schoonover's engagement was broken within a year, the murals are still there. Indeed, Hugh Roberts' courthouse is presently being restored under the auspices of the National Trust for Historic Preservation and is listed in the *Register of Historic Buildings* issued by the Department of the Interior.

Pike County, Pennsylvania

1914 was a momentous year for "F. E." as Schoonover was becoming known. On January 5 his only son, Cortlandt, was born; and on May 16 he bought his place in Bushkill, Pike County, Pennsylvania—the land of his forebears.

The area provided him with every prop needed to turn out a prodigious amount of book and magazine material. According to his diary, the morning after Schoonover bought his place in Bushkill, he rose at 3:30 A.M., cooked his breakfast, and left the house for a walking trip to the ridge of Simon Mountain which rose from the back edge of a field adjacent to his new property. The ridge was a narrow plateau that Will and Amos, the Eshbach brothers, had cleared to create two farms on some of the least valuable ground in the Pocono Mountain area. The artist followed the Eshbachs' road, for his mission was to see about manure for a garden and to talk Will Eshbach into throwing his plow on a wagon load of what was really a poor mixture of straw and droppings.

Frank Schoonover's garden was one of his prides. He carefully drew plans for the layout and kept records on the types and growth details of the seeds. He believed in the adage from Amos Bronson Alcott's *Tablets* that "Who loves a garden still his Eden keeps, still perennial pleasures plants, and wholesome harvests reaps."

The Bushkill Elementals

He was fascinated by the "Bushkill elementals," as he called men like Will and Amos. They peopled his illustrations with a tremendous vigor and a strength that was an identifying characteristic of his work. They all called him "Frank" and would do anything for him. Not caring to understand his life style, they nonetheless had a deep respect for him and took tremendous pride in identifying themselves in his pictures.

Bushkill Landing on the Delaware River, *oil on canvas,*
12" x 16". From A Journal of Public Policy in the Delaware
Valley, *"Tock's Island Dam," Vol. 1, No. 9, October 1975.*

Schoonover, like a number of great illustrators, had one model that stood out. James Montgomery Flagg ingeniously employed himself; Howard Pyle had John Weller; J. C. Leyendecker's man was Charles Beach. These models were major characters in the drama of art. Frank Schoonover had perhaps the most remarkable of all: he was Will Eshbach's son, Russell.

Russ was strapping and ruggedly picturesque with a deep-furrow stride. He did naturally, with awesome vigor and strength, almost everything Frank Schoonover was called on by his publishers to put into his pictures. Russ could fight. When he played Sunday baseball for the Bushkill league in the Pocono Circuit, Russ would get into a fight almost every game, and he played the game with his fists almost as well as with his mouth.

Frank told Russ how he was going to rent the second floor of Hemingway's Mill for a studio. Would Russ help him set it up and pose?

"I can't stand still like that, Frank, and you know it. Besides, I've got work I've promised," was Russ's response.

"You can pose for me on your way to work, Russ, and make as much in an hour or two as you can make for the whole rest of the day; and I'll teach you the easy way to hold still for a while, and that's all I will have to teach you."

"You mean you'll start your day same time as the rest of us, and not like I hear about those other painter fellows?"

"Yes, and rainy days too, Russ. Don't forget you haven't been making much on rainy days, and I know money freezes up in Bushkill in the winter. You could save what you make from me and that would carry you and Will both all winter."

Russ did not know it, but he was facing the first in a pattern of decisions that would make him a rich and famous man. Schoonover was offering him a priceless opportunity in exchange for very little effort on his part. Just a short walk down a hill and only the ability to hold still while his features became known nationwide.

It wasn't long before a magazine cover hit Bushkill, and there was Russ Eshbach as a Royal Canadian Mountie. Through Schoonover's portrayal of him (he posed for all of Schoonover's World War pictures), Russ was getting a pre-TV media exposure in 10,000,000 magazines and books each month from 1915 through the 1920s. It is hard to estimate the number of readers who saw Russ each month, but a joke of Schoonover's was that when he picked up a magazine with Russ Eshbach's picture in it, he could be sure the picture was a Schoonover.

Today the Honorable Russell Eshbach, retired Pennsylvania legislator, still robust and barrel-chested, credits Frank Schoonover's recognition of him for a successful life.

The Twenties

During the 1920s, Schoonover was undoubtedly at the height of his production. This was an era when children were brought up on beautifully illustrated classics. Nowadays good copies of these books fetch five to 10 times their original prices if in good condition, and even for that money they are hard to find.

In 1921 alone, Schoonover illustrated 14 books, interspersed with magazine stories and serials. Many of the titles are classics: *Treasure Island* by Robert Louis Stevenson; *The Arabian Nights Entertainment; Robinson Crusoe* by Daniel Defoe; *Lafayette* by Lucy Foster Madison; *Hans Andersen's Fairy Tales* by Hans Christian Andersen; *Kidnapped* by Robert Louis Stevenson; *The Swiss Family Robinson* by David Wyss; *Robin Hood* by Sir Walter Scott; *Gulliver's Travels* by Jonathan Swift; and *Grimm's Fairy Tales* by Jakob and Wilhelm Grimm.

One of Schoonover's favorite phrases was "the beefsteak house," which meant any good restaurant. When in New York delivering one of his pictures, he would almost always plan to stay the night to carry out the strategy of "the beefsteak house." This was

Frank Schoonover's Bushkill, Penn-
sylvania studio on the second floor of
Hemingway's Mill. Photographed
by Schoonover, 1915.
Courtesy Private Collection.

Russ Eshbach—Schoonover's
Number 1 model. Courtesy
The Honorable J. Russell Eshbach.

Treasure Island, *oil on canvas, 36" x 25". From* Treasure Island *by Robert Louis Stevenson, jacket illustration, Harper & Brothers, 1921.*

a well-planned maneuver. Upon acceptance of the picture by the art editor of, say, *Harper's* or *Scribner's*, Schoonover would learn from him the name of the man who would be doing the engraving, and immediately invite him to "the beefsteak house." You might consider this bribery, but the engraver could make the painting captivate the reader or he could, as would sometimes happen even under the best circumstances, ruin a picture's effectiveness. F. E. claimed he never had an enemy among the engravers.

He did a lot of books for Harper's. One Thursday he got a call from the editor asking if he could expect an important picture due the next day. How had it been shipped and when?

Schoonover had not even stretched the canvas, but told the editor everything was coming along fine.

"That's not what I asked you, F. E."

"You'll have the finished product tomorrow afternoon."

"You know it has to go to the engraver tomorrow. Have you even started it?"

"I told you it's coming along." Schoonover put a brushstroke on a piece of canvas. "Yes, and I'll have it in your hands late Friday afternoon; wait for me."

"Well, I still don't think you've started it."

"I have."

"See you tomorrow with the finished picture, and it had better be good."

The editor hung up and told his secretary, "Schoonover's as good a liar as he is an artist. Hasn't even started that picture, but I'll bet on its being here."

Schoonover worked all night and almost until train time the next day. He delivered the painting as promised and went to "the beefsteak house" with the engraver.

Zane Grey

Zane Grey as late as 1970 was still known as "the world's most successful author." His first magazine story was "A Day on the Delaware" (tales of freshwater fishing), published by *Recreation Magazine* in 1902. Schoonover illustrated a number of Zane Grey's serials including *Open Range, Avalanche,* and *Rustlers of Silver River,* and books including *Rogue River Feud* and *Valley of Wild Horses.*

Both men were great fishermen, although Grey was very keen on salt-water fishing and Schoonover liked fresh water. They enjoyed each other's company and Grey liked the illustrations that Schoonover took great pride in producing for his colorful stories. Both enjoyed fantastic exposure during the '20s when both were at their productive peaks. It is impossible to establish any realistic figures on the amount of Grey's monthly output, but we do know that Schoonover's reproductions for his works reached upwards of 5,000,000 readers a month. Cumulative reader involvement would probably have put this figure conservatively at around 10,000,000 a month. Considering then the circulation of the magazine- and book-reading public, this was big league.

By the 1930s, production of this type was no longer bearable. I remember my father's story about his decision to switch to other forms of art expression (in which the killing deadlines of illustration were not present), although he still did a great deal of illustrating. Schoonover switched to landscapes. He really enjoyed doing landscapes—for the next 35 years!

The Man

Frank Schoonover was a legend of self-discipline. His dress and grooming were immaculate. There is a famous photograph of him outside his tent in the winter of 1904 above the Arctic Circle where he is sporting a handsome bow tie and his best gray flannel shirt and waistcoat (see page 22). His magnificent attire was not for a pose; it was perfectly natural for Frank Schoonover—absolutely in character. He was seldom seen without a tie, even when wearing his painting smock in the studio, and his initials, F. E. S., were invariably embroidered on the cuffs of his smock.

Models in Western costumes, photographed by Schoonover in the 1920s. Courtesy Private Collection.

Schoonover started his working day no later than eight in the morning, carried lunch to his studio, and usually worked steadily until five in the afternoon. Oddly enough, Schoonover's studio was not aesthetic. It was crowded with artifacts, and the enormous production of his works often seemed to create a clutter. But he could easily zero in on a particular painting in a stack of canvases or retrieve a needed object instantly. His photographic memory had stacked it away. His thinking and mental order were akin to his self-discipline.

It was his habit to walk to and from work even long after he owned an automobile. He ate supper almost invariably at six, and there were not many evenings when he did not rise from the dining-room table and go to his drawing board where he thought nothing of turning out at least three or four pen-and-inks finished for publication. If he varied this routine, it was usually to make sketches for his next day's work or to read galley proofs for selection of illustration subjects.

However, all was not work for the artist. He was an incurable ham and "interview" was his favorite game. He imitated W. C. Fields at every opportunity and finally had his voice and mannerisms so honed that it all came out as natural.

He also painted vivid portraits in words. He recalled the noted American impressionist painter Edward Redfield. "I remember Redfield well—used to live in the Peter House, that was the village hotel in Bushkill, Pennsylvania, in the winter and called himself a 'Winter Painter'—never painted in the summer—claimed it was too damn green. He knew how to paint snow though. He taught me to mix in just a bit of vermilion. How much? Well, he'd split a short stick down from the top a little and stick in a piece of white paper. Then he would put the stick in the snow. With that you could see the contrast of color in the snow. When he started a picture in the morning he always lay the shadows in first. Then though they changed during the day he could come back to them. Redfield used a lot of paint. When he was through there was always a ring of tubes around his easel."

Schoonover's father, Brevet Colonel John Schoonover, lived in the Peters House, and one night Redfield set his day's work on a chair and said, "Colonel, how much do you think I could get for that picture in Philadelphia?"

"Well," said the Colonel, "it's got $150 worth of paint on it."

Schoonover Red

Legend has it that Schoonover was fascinated by the color red. He used a special mixture of cadmium red to which he added a touch of varnish for brilliance. A spot of what came to be known as "Schoonover Red" seemed to appear in some form in all of his pictures—a sash, a shirt, buttons, a knife blade, a sail, a blanket. In fact, one way of spotting "a Schoonover" is to look for this characteristic touch of red.

It tickled my father, when on landscape, to carry a little camp axe he had had with him on the winter expedition in Canada, and to cut a blaze where he had worked. He would paint the blaze "Schoonover Red." It gave him great pleasure to show off old blazes when traveling around the country.

Public Service

Under Pyle's tutelage, Schoonover had early learned how to live his life with gusto. His artistic, literary, religious, theatrical, and social interests were part of his life style, as well as his work. He joined clubs and organizations, always as an active member.

It was only natural that Wilmington, Delaware, the hometown of the illustrator, should be the major focus of his community efforts. A dedicated Episcopalian, he regularly attended Immanuel Church services, served on the Vestry as Senior Warden for 40 years, and designed a variety of stained-glass windows. He and his Brandywine colleagues were active in the Wilmington Society of the Fine Arts and the Wilmington

Hemingway's Pond, Bushkill, Pennsylvania,
oil on canvas, 28" x 32", painted in 1947.
Courtesy Hotel Du Pont, Wilmington, Delaware.

Sketch Club. Howard Pyle had started an exclusive club termed Quill and Grill, which brought the artist in touch with well-established literary and art personages, as well as men in business and financial circles. Schoonover was a great admirer of Abraham Lincoln, so the Lincoln Club, for which he designed the insignia, brought him much pleasure. He was the prime force behind the establishment of the Delaware Art Museum and their ownership of the world's greatest collection of Howard Pyle's work and the Bancroft Collection of Pre-Raphaelites.

In Philadelphia memberships and honors came to him from the Racquet Club, the Franklin Inn Club, The Loyal Legion of the United States Commandery of the State of Pennsylvania, the Art Alliance, and the Philadelphia Academy of the Fine Arts.

When in New York the illustrator spent time at the Players Club, the Salmagundi Club, and the Society of Illustrators. As a guest he was often included in meetings of the Explorer's Club.

Honors and Exhibitions

Throughout his career and lifetime Frank Schoonover received many honors and awards and his work has been exhibited from Wilmington to the Kremlin. In 1962 he was called "Dean of Delaware Artists" by the Wilmington press. In that same year the Wilmington Society of the Fine Arts set up a retrospective one-man exhibition of Schoonover's works. The Society holds a number of his paintings and illustrated books in the permanent museum collection and library. He is represented in the permanent collection of the Brandywine Museum, where the most comprehensive collection of his illustrated books is housed.

Three years of correspondence between Rockwell Kent (who spent several years in

Fireplace in the Rodney Street studio. Photographed by the artist in 1915. Courtesy Private Collection.

Portrait of Frank Schoonover in a Howard Pyle smock, 1920. (Mrs. Pyle embroidered the smocks even to the artists' initials on the cuffs.) Courtesy Private Collection.

Schoonover at work on Polytechnical Mural, *oil on canvas, 7' x 24', 1938. Courtesy H. Fletcher Brown Vocational High School, Wilmington Public Schools.*

Artist with young student. Photographed by Frank Herzog, 1952, in the artist's studio, Wilmington, Delaware.

Frank E. Schoonover and a bust of him created by Kate Doetz of Wilmington,
Delaware, 1962, bronze, life-size. Courtesy Private Collection.

Reflections of an artist—at 88

The paddle dips softly but firmly into the still waters of the Delaware River. A nostalgic smile flickers across the face of the white-thatched canoeist who knows and has painted every cove and trail of Pennsylvania's Bushkill country. Frank E. Schoonover, dean of Delaware artists who is 88 tomorrow still journeys frequently to the scenes of his youth. "As a boy I used to spend the summers here with my grandmother," he muses. His eyes grow wistful as he recalls his growing fondness for the Pike County wilds where, later, he met his life's mate, Martha Culbertson of Philadelphia, who died Sunday. This loss was imminent but not anticipated three weeks ago when the artist and his son, Cortlandt (Pat) made the canoe trip recorded here. It is the family's wish that the pre-planned birthday salute to Schoonover should appear "as a tribute to Mother." Although near 90, "The Dean" remains active as a teacher and an exhibitor, working from his studio at 1616 N. Rodney St. But there's a corner of the Poconos' Bushkill country that is forever Schoonover's. His Pike County studio-retreat is a mail order, high-ceilinged barn. "Before that I rented a room over a sawmill. It was all right except when they ran the saw," he recollects." Then it shook the whole building." But the hand that wields the brush — and paddle — is as steady today as 60 years ago when the art world was just beginning to hear of Frank E. Schoonover. The deftly-sketched canoe is his trademark and the key to his personality.

Schoonover's trademark, varied according to use. Courtesy Private Collection.

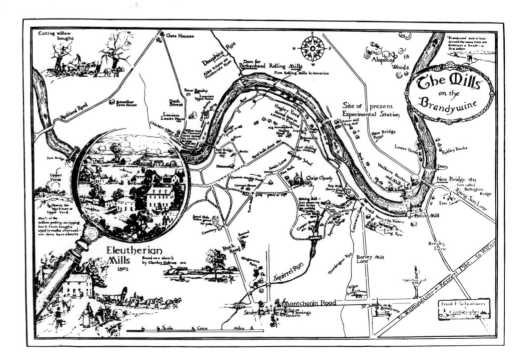

The Mills on the Brandywine, *pen and ink on board, 11" x 16½".*
Endpapers for DuPont: The Autobiography of an American Enterprise, *by E. I. du Pont de Nemours & Company, Wilmington, Delaware. Charles Scribner's Sons, New York, 1952. Courtesy E. I. du Pont de Nemours & Company, Inc.*

Russia), the Russian Minister of Art, and the author has indicated that there are paintings of Frank Schoonover's displayed in the Kremlin. (I have an amusing letter from the Russian minister, written to Kent shortly before his death, that advised patience in our investigation because "the art removed from Russia by Napoleon has not yet been returned.") Two large mural paintings now believed to be in the Kremlin were confiscated from the du Pont residence in Cardenas, Cuba, by Fidel Castro.

Teaching

For many years, F. E. had based his own work on the tenet that imagination is the key to reality. In 1942 he felt it was time to pass on a few of his secrets of success as Mr. Pyle had done for him. In short, he started teaching. He disliked the phrase "art school" and established his program of "art classes" that were to continue for the rest of his working life.

He was especially happy with children and catered to a group of them on Saturday mornings. Next dearest to his heart after the children was a special class composed of ready-to-retire, retired, or just people seeking further fulfillment of their lives. Of course, Schoonover also had a class of "hard-core" art students. But he maintained the humanistic approach and avoided as best he could the "art school" concept.

The Artist

Although oils, pen-and-inks, photography, and teaching were his forte and pleasure, he was an accomplished watercolorist, restorer, portraitist, and muralist, and he took particular pride in his skill as a cartographer. Along the way, he created bookplates, etchings, collector's plates, and even a statue of an Indian.

He was a master letterer, and took great pride in his penmanship. Crayon, charcoal and pencil drawings by him are superb. His lantern slides, often hand-colored, earned him a professional reputation in this medium alone. He wrote and illustrated stories for *Scribner's, Harper's, American Boy,* and a number of other magazines, traveling and photographing as he went. The Museum of the Wilmington Savings Fund Society held a one-man show of his photography as recently as 1974.

But how would the artist himself, looking over his 95 years, have felt about his achievement. I believe he got the greatest joy out of his proficiency in portraying the beauty of action. "A picture has got to tell a story," he would tell his students over and over again. Into the cloth of his story-pictures he wove the vibrant threads of action. The vitality of his interpretation of the outdoors gave his art a very special individuality.

Shortly before he died, he turned to me one day with his mischievous smile beaming and said, "You can spot a Schoonover every time; even I can."

Poster for Scribner's Magazine, *oil on canvas, 24" x 18", July 1903. Courtesy Private Collection.*

THE FRONTIER

CAPTURING OUTDOOR SCENES OF ACTION WAS FRANK SCHOONOVER'S
NATURAL DELIGHT—AND THE DELIGHT OF HIS VAST PUBLIC. THE
WESTERN UNITED STATES AND CANADA WAS SCHOONOVER'S FAVOR-
ITE SETTING. HE HAD SPENT A GREAT DEAL OF TIME THERE: ON
HORSEBACK WITH THE COWBOYS; TRAVELING THOUSANDS OF MILES
BY CANOE, DOGSLED, AND SNOWSHOE WITH THE INDIANS; AND
TREKKING MANY LONG MILES AFOOT. HE BECAME A MAGICIAN OF
DRAMATIC OUTDOOR COMPOSITION AND ALWAYS HAD HIS PUBLIC
EAGERLY ANTICIPATING THE NEXT PICTORIAL ADVENTURE.

Hopalong Takes Command, *oil on canvas, 30" x 20". From* Outing Magazine, *"The Fight at Buckskin" by Clarence E. Mulford, July, 1905. Collection Delaware Art Museum.*

The Oregon Trail of 1843, *oil on canvas. 21″ x 30″.*
From The Rolling Wheels *by Katherine Grey.*
Little, Brown, 1937. Collection Mrs. Harry W. Lynch.

Tex and Patches, *oil on canvas, 36" x 27". Colt Patent Firearms Company poster, November, 1926. Collection John and Lucy Epstein.*

Old Man by the Horse, *oil on canvas, 24" x 24". From* American Boy Magazine, *"Giddap" by John A. Moroso. January, 1915. Collection Mr. and Mrs. Thomas Spackman.*

Three Cowpunchers, *oil on canvas, 30" x 20". From* The Bar-20 Three *By Clarence E. Mulford,*
A.C. McClurg, 1921. Collection Delaware Art Museum.

The Fight on the Desert, *oil on canvas, 30" x 38". From* Youth's Companion, *"Gun Runners" by Edwin Cole, 1926. Courtesy Private Collection.*

Wheat, *oil on canvas, 33" x 30". From* Country Gentleman, *"Wheat" by Robert W. Ritchie, November, 1924. Collection M. Knoedler & Company, Inc.*

Shorty Has the Best Position, *oil on canvas, 30" x 20". From* Outing Magazine, *"The Fight at Buckskin"*
by Clarence E. Mulford, 1905; also used in The Bar-20 Three *by Clarence E. Mulford, A.C. McClurg, 1921.*
Collection Mr. and Mrs. James C. Engman. Photograph courtesy of the Brandywine Museum.

On Leapt the Canoe like a Runaway, *oil on canvas, 48" x 32". From* Redbook Magazine, *"Valley of Voices" by George T. Marsh, August, 1924. Courtesy Private Collection.*

Buffalo Hunt, *oil on canvas, 34" x 36". From* American Boy Magazine, *"Beaver Woman" by James W. Schultz, 1935. Courtesy Private Collection.*

Buffao Hunt, *oil on canvas, 34" x 37". From* American Boy Magazine, *"Beaver Woman" by James W. Schultz, 1935. Courtesy Private Collection.*

The Deer Stalker, *oil on canvas, 44" x 36". From* American Boy Magazine, *"The Warring Tribes"*
by James W. Schultz, January, 1920. Courtesy of Marian Stein, New York, New York.

The Maid of the Forest, *oil on canvas, 40" x 36". From* The Maid of the Forest *by Randall Parrish, A.C. McClurg, June, 1913. Collection Delaware Art Museum.*

Indian in Canoe, *oil on canvas, 36" x 30". From* Ladies Home Journal, *cover illustration, December, 1922. Courtesy Private Collection.*

Fishing from a Canoe, *oil on board, 20″ x 16″. From* The Curious Career of Roderick Campbell
by Jean N. McIlwraith, Houghton Mifflin, 1901.

Trader and Imperial Scout,
oil on canvas, 30" x 40".
From American Red Cross Magazine
for "Trader and Imperial Scout"
by Constance Lindsay Skinner, August 1932.
Courtesy of Robert G. Hackett.

Indian Leading Captive, *oil on canvas, 36" x 30".* From To Have and to Hold *by Mary Johnston, Houghton Mifflin, 1931.*

Ojibway Indian Spearing the Maskenozha (Pike), *oil on canvas, 30" x 40". From* Popular Magazine, *cover illustration, December 2, 1923; also used for* Frontier Day *edited by Oliver G. Swan, Grosset & Dunlap, 1928. Courtesy Private Collection.*

*Inscription by George Marsh to F.E.S.
in a copy of* The Whelps of the Wolf, *1922.
Courtesy Private Collection.*

The Whelps of the Wolf,
oil on canvas, 36″ x 30″.
From The Whelps of the Wolf,
cover illustration by George Marsh,
Penn Publishing Company, 1922.
The Permanent Collection
of the University of Delaware.

Escape from Forest Fire, *oil on canvas, 36" x 26".* From Popular Magazine, *cover illustration, November 7, 1920. Courtesy of Robert G. Hackett.*

The Sixth Charge Was Closer, *oil on canvas, 34" x 36". From* American Boy Magazine, *"Stained Gold" by James Willard Schultz, September 1927. Courtesy Private Collection.*

The Appearance of the Great Chief Dark Horse Stopped the Action, *oil on canvas, 30" x 21". From* Rolling Wheels *by Katherine Grey. Courtesy Private Collection.*

Indian Leaving the Haunted Forest, *oil on canvas, 30" x 40". From* American Boy Magazine, *"The Voice from the Hills" by Frank Hendryx, July 1921. Courtesy Private Collection.*

Mackenzie and Indian Boy, *oil on canvas, 30" x 36". From* American Boy Magazine, *"The Men Who Went Down" by Laurie Yoek Erskine, February 1921. Courtesy the Glenbow-Alberta Institute, Calgary, Alberta, Canada.*

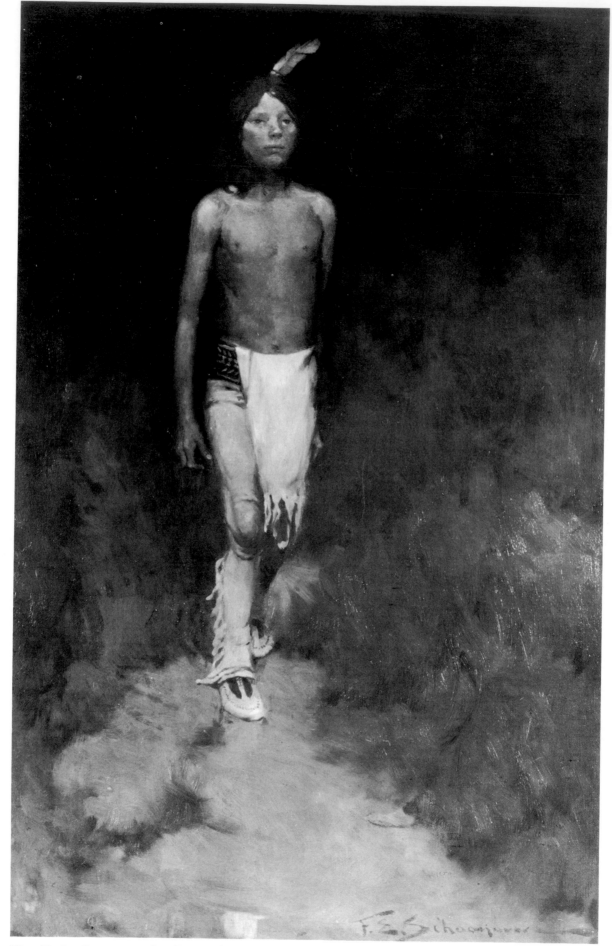

Silver Heels, *oil on canvas, 22″ x 16″. From* Harper's Magazine, *"Cardigan" by Robert W. Chambers, September 14, 1901. Courtesy Private Collection.*

Preparing for the Buffalo Hunt, *oil on canvas, 32" x 13". From* American Boy Magazine,
"Beaver Woman" by James Willard Schultz, September 1935. Courtesy Private Collection.

"Ho, it bends well," said Kawakiam, *oil on canvas, 21" x 30". From* The Boy Captive of Old Deerfield
by Mary P. Wells Smith, Little, Brown & Co., 1929.

The Factor's Indian Wife and Child, *ink and watercolor, 16" x 29". from* Harper's Magazine, *"The Fur Harvesters"*
by Frank E. Schoonover, October 1912. Courtesy the Glenbow-Alberta Institute, Calgary, Alberta, Canada.

Indian Entering Grand Battery, *oil on board, 12″ x 16″. From* McClure's Magazine, *"Colonial Fighters at Louisburg" by Cyrus Townsend Brady, September 1901. Courtesy Private Collection.*

Trapper Trapped, *pencil and charcoal on board, 36" x 30". From* Century Magazine, *"Sentinels of the Silence" by Agnes Dean Cameron, December 1909. Courtesy Robert G. Hackett.*

Girl with Man in Canoe Firing Gun, *oil on canvas, 24" x 50". From* Red Book Magazine, *"Wolf Pass" by William Byron Mowery, May 1930. Courtesy Private Collection.*

I Got My Far Seeing Instrument and with It Covered Them, *oil on canvas, 36" x 34". From* American Boy Magazine, *"Skull Head the Terrible" by James Willard Schultz, July 1929. Courtesy Robert G. Hackett.*

Lone Hand, *oil on canvas, 33" x 30 1/8". From* Popular Magazine, *cover and illustration for "The Lone Hand"*
by Francis Lynde, February 18, 1928. Collection M. Knoedler and Company, Inc.

The Rescue, *oil on board, 20" x 16". From* The Curious Career of Roderick Campbell *by Jean M. McIlwraith, Houghton Mifflin, 1901.*

You're a Big Target, Jim, *oil on canvas, 29" x 36". From* Country Gentleman, *"Moon Mountain" January, 1927. Courtesy Private Collection.*

Tucker Hotel, *oil on canvas, 30" x 36". From* American Boy Magazine, *"The Man Who Was Wanted" by Laurie York Erskine, March 1927. Courtesy Private Collection.*

Mount at the Fair, *oil on board, 20" x 16". From* Cardigan *by Robert W. Chambers,*
Harper & Brothers, 1901. Courtesy Private Collection.

The Dog Fight, *oil on canvas, 25" x 30". From* Country Gentleman, *"Cowards Both" by Albert Payson Terhune, February 1926.*

Sockeye, *oil on canvas, 24" x 30". From* Country Gentleman, *"The Singing River" by Zane Grey, 1929.*

"See here, Rollins," Black said brusquely, "no irons needed on this boy," *oil on canvas, 35" x 76".*
From Country Gentleman, *"Rustlers of Silver River" by Zane Grey, January 1930. Courtesy Private Collection.*

Masked Indian Dancer, *oil on canvas, 27" x 38". From* American Boy Magazine, *"Beaver Woman" by James Willard Schultz, August 1935. Courtesy Private Collection.*

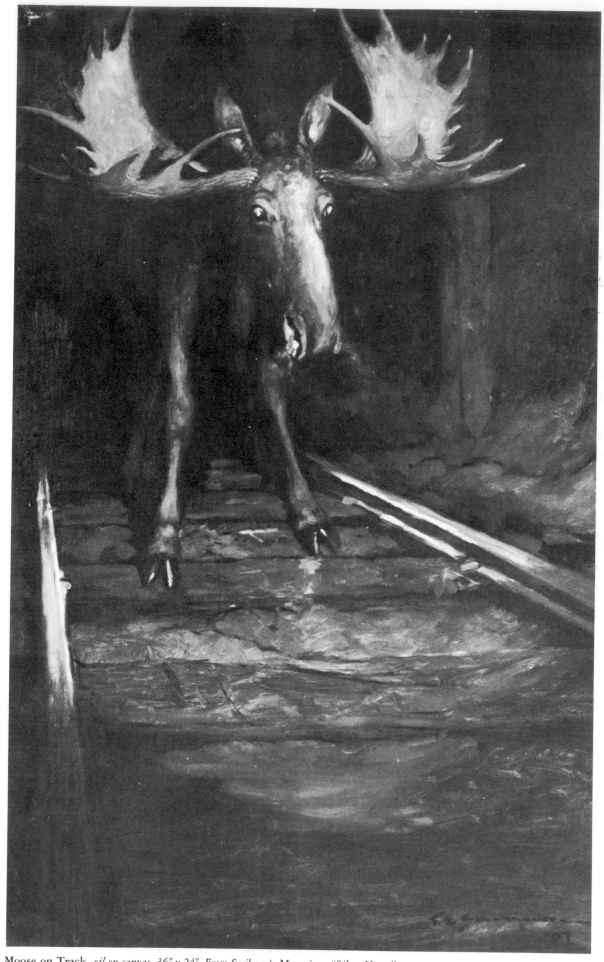

Moose on Track, *oil on canvas, 36" x 24". From* Scribner's Magazine, *"Silver Horns"*
by Henry Van Dyke, April 1907. Courtesy Private Collection.

The Black Fox Den, *oil on canvas, 30" x 40". From* American Boy Magazine, *"Voice from the Hills" by James B. Hendryx, August 1921.*

Girl with Rifle, *oil on canvas, 34" x 32". From* American Boy Magazine, *"The Clear Course" by Albert Richard Wetjen, 1926.*

The Trailmakers, *oil on canvas, 29 1/2" x 42". Calendar for the Dupont Company, May, 1941.*

Wa-Gush, *oil on canvas, 30" x 48". From* Outing Magazine, *"Wa-Gush" by Lawrence Mott, August, 1906; also used in* The Edge of Wilderness *by Frank E. Schoonover, Methuen Publications, 1974.*

Death Rapids, *oil on canvas, 36" x 27". From* The Whelps of the Wolf *by George Marsh, Penn Publishing Company, 1922.*
The Permanent Collection of the University of Delaware. Photograph Courtesy the Brandywine Museum.

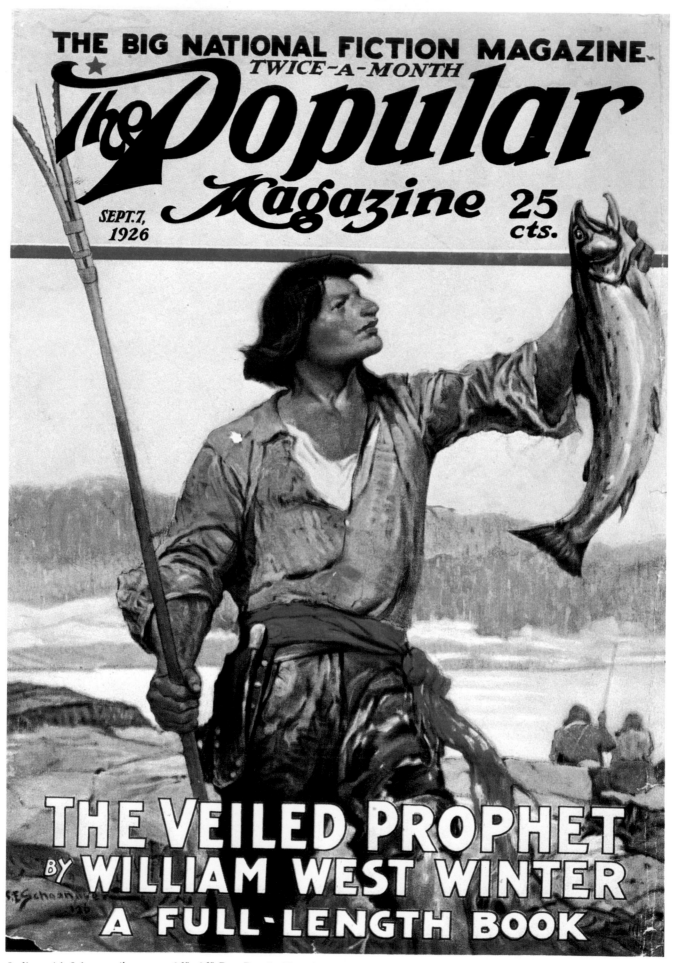

Indian with Salmon, *oil on canvas, 36" x 26". From* Popular Magazine, *September, 1926. Courtesy Private Collection.*

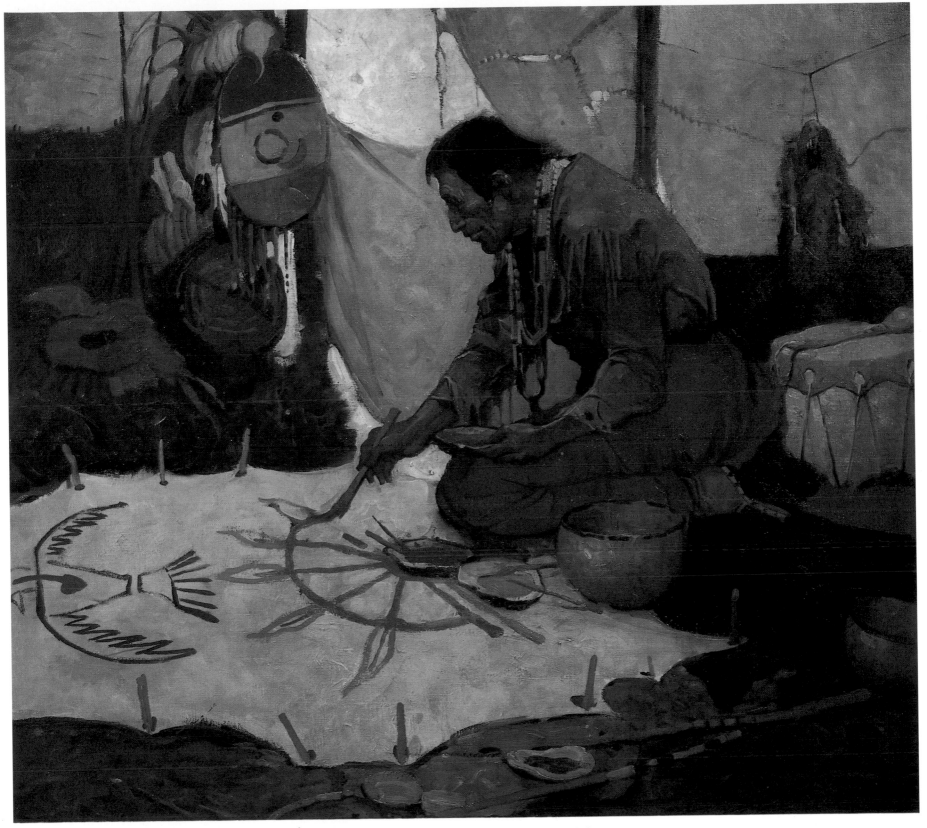

The Indian Sun Priest, *oil on canvas, 30″ x 34″. From* American Boy Magazine, *"Red Crow's Brother" by James W. Schultz, 1927; also used in* The Edge of Wilderness *by Frank E. Schoonover, Methuen Publications, 1974. Collection Delaware Art Museum.*

Trapper with Christmas Tree, *oil on canvas, 36″ x 25″. From* Popular Magazine, *cover illustration, December, 1923; also used in* The Edge of Wilderness *by Frank E. Schoonover, Methuen Publications, 1974.*

Great Sachem from the South, *oil on canvas, 30" x 46". From* Redbook, *"Valley of Voices" by George T. Marsh, serialized in 1924. Courtesy Private Collection.*

Let Go of Me, Winkler, *oil on canvas, 26" x 38". From* Country Gentlemen, *"The Debt" by Sewell P. Wright, February, 1931. Courtesy Private Collection.*

The Freezing Man Was Dragged to Safety, *oil on canvas, 40" x 32". From* Scribner's Magazine,
"When the Prince Came Home" by George T. Marsh, May, 1974. Courtesy Private Collection.

Snowblind, *oil on canvas, 40" x 32". From* Scribner's Magazine, *"When the Prince Came Home" by George T. Marsh, 1914; also used in* The Edge of Wilderness *by Frank E. Schoonover, Methuen Publications, 1974. Collection Kenneth H. Newbould.*

The Mirage, *oil on canvas, 34" x 30". From* American Boy Magazine, *August, 1920. Courtesy Private Collection.*

The Wagon Train, *oil on canvas, 54 1/2" x 54 1/2". From* Country Gentleman, *"Mighty Horizon" by George T. Marsh, May, 1936.*

Colt Patent Firearms Posters, *proposed drawings, oil on gesso board, 14" x 12", 1926. Courtesy Private Collection.*

Playing Cards in Tent, *oil on canvas, 20" x 30". From Scribner's Magazine, "The Edge of Wilderness" by Frank E. Schoonover, April, 1905. Courtesy the Glenbow-Alberta Institute, Calgary, Alberta, Canada.*

The Poor Buildings at Midnight Bay *(also called* Christmas on the Klondike*), oil on canvas, 32" x 42". From* Country Gentleman, *"The Valley Beyond" by William B. Mowery, April, 1938. Collection Lewis S. Black.*

Frank Schoonover Leading Guide on Portage, *lantern slide, unpublished, 1911. Courtesy Private Collection.*

Two Canoes and Indians Coming Ashore, *Long Lake, Ontario, Canada, lantern slide, 1911. Courtesy Private Collection.*

Portrait of Ojibway Indian Chief *near Long Lake, Ontario, Canada, lantern slide by Frank Schoonover, 4" x 4", 1911. Courtesy Private Collection.*

The Cree Chief, *wash on board, 16" x 18", 1912. Courtesy Sewell C. Biggs Private Collection.*

Stretching the White Buffalo Skin, *oil on canvas, 36" x 24". From* American Boy Magazine, *July 1935. Courtesy Sewell C. Biggs Private Collection.*

Return of Ancient Otter, *oil on canvas, 36" x 27".* From American Boy Magazine, *"The White Blackfoot" by James Willard Schultz, July 1918. Collection Frank Harding. Photograph courtesy the Brandywine River Museum.*

Breaking Trail, *oil on canvas, 26" x 48". From* Red Book Magazine, *"Valley of Voices" by George Marsh, May 1924; also used in* The Edge of Wilderness *by Frank E. Schoonover, Methuen Publications, 1974.*

Lead Sled Dog, *oil on canvas, 27" x 34". From American Boy Magazine, "The Warring Tribes" by James Willard Schultz, March 1920.*
Courtesy the Glenbow-Alberta Institute, Calgary, Alberta, Canada.

Belinda Looked down Her Narrow Nose and Gave a Soft Blast of Derision, *oil on canvas, 26" x 35". From* American Boy Magazine,
"The Goat Getters" by Herbert Evans, January 1929. Courtesy Private Collection.

Pack of Running Wolves, *oil on canvas, 30" x 30". From* American Boy Magazine, *"Hide Rack Stands By," February 1934. Courtesy Private Collection.*

In the Whirling Blizzard, *oil on canvas, 34" x 22". From* American Boy Magazine, *"Connie Morgan" by James B. Hendryx, August 1920. Courtesy Private Collection.*

Men Pulling Sled in Arctic, *oil on canvas, 24" x 43". From* Collier's Magazine, *"Survival" by Charles Selby, May 15, 1926. Courtesy Private Collection.*

Pulling the Sledge, *oil on canvas, 22" x 14". From* Scribner's Magazine, *1903; also used in* The Blood Lilies
by W. A. Fraser, William Biggs, 1903. Courtesy Private Collection.

The Struggle in the Storm, *oil on canvas, 22" x 14". From* Scribner's Magazine, *1903; also used in* The Blood Lilies *by W. A. Fraser, William Biggs, 1903. Courtesy Private Collection.*

The Capture, *oil on canvas, 27" x 18": From* Bobby of the Labrador *by Dillon Wallace,*
A. C. McClurg, 1916. Courtesy Private Collection.

Trapper and Dog Team, *oil on canvas, 36" x 34". From* Country Gentleman, *cover illustration, February 1937.*
Courtesy Permanent Collection Wilmington Trust Company, Wilmington, Delaware.

CLASSICS AND HISTORY

A CLASSIC, ILLUSTRATED BY ONE OF THE GREAT ILLUSTRATORS, WAS A TRADITIONAL CHRISTMAS GIFT IN THE FIRST HALF OF THE CENTURY. CHILDREN GREW UP ON THESE BEAUTIFUL BOOKS AND WORE THEM OUT—LITERALLY. FRANK SCHOONOVER'S EDITIONS WERE PARTICULARLY POPULAR. THE SUBJECTS WERE MOSTLY HISTORICAL—REAL OR IMAGINARY—RANGING FROM LUCY FOSTER MADISON'S *LINCOLN* TO SIR WALTER SCOTT'S *IVANHOE*. SCHOONOVER'S OTHER HISTORICAL CLASSICS ARE LIKE THE SUMMER READING LIST THAT USED TO BE PART OF SCHOOLING: *THE CHILDREN'S LONGFELLOW, A JERSEY BOY IN THE REVOLUTION, TALES FROM SHAKESPEARE, ROBINSON CRUSOE, LAFAYETTE, WASHINGTON, KIDNAPPED, HANS ANDERSEN'S FAIRY TALES, THE ARABIAN NIGHT'S ENTERTAINMENT, TREASURE ISLAND, ROBIN HOOD, GULLIVER'S TRAVELS, KING ARTHUR AND HIS KNIGHTS,* AND DOZENS OF OTHERS.

Revolutionary War Hero, *oil on canvas, 36" x 36". From* Popular Magazine, *cover illustration, February, 1930. Collection Delaware Art Museum.*

Drummer Boy, *oil on canvas, 36" x 24", unpublished, 1899.*

On George's Fourth Birthday His Father Bought Him a Pony, *oil on canvas, 36" x 30".*
From Washington *by Lucy F. Madison, Penn Publishing Company, 1925. Courtesy Private Collection.*

The Spirit of the Colonists, *oil on canvas, 36" x 30". From* Washington *by Lucy F. Madison,*
Penn Publishing Company, 1925. Collection Mrs. Harry W. Lynch, Wilmington, Delaware.

Lafayette, *oil on canvas, 36" x 29". From* Lafayette *by Lucy F. Madison, Penn Publishing Company, 1921.*
Collection Mr. Harry W. Lynch, Jr., Wilmington, Delaware.

The Prison Cell Seemed More Dismal than Ever, *oil on canvas, 36" x 30". From* Lafayette
by Lucy F. Madison, Penn Publishing Company, 1921. Courtesy Private Collection.

Evangeline, *oil on canvas. 36" x 30". From* Evangeline *by Henry Wadsworth Longfellow,*
Houghton Mifflin, 1908. Courtesy Private Collection.

Ivanhoe, *oil on canvas, 36" x 30". From* Ivanhoe *by Sir Walter Scott, Harper & Brothers, 1922. Collection St. Andrew's School.*

Isaac of York and Rebecca, *oil on canvas, 36" x 30". From* Ivanhoe *by Sir Walter Scott, Harper & Brothers, 1922. Collection St. Andrew's School.*

The Friar and the Knight, *oil on canvas, 36" x 30". From* Ivanhoe *by Sir Walter Scott, Harper & Brothers, 1922. Collection St. Andrew's School.*

Aladdin and the Genie, *oil on canvas. 36" x 28". From* The Arabian Nights Entertainment, *jacket illustration, Harper & Brothers, 1921. Courtesy Anonymous Lender.*

Attack on Indiamen by the Pickering, *oil on canvas, 36" x 30". From* American Boy Magazine, *serialized; also used in* Privateers of '76 *by Ralph D. Paine, Penn Publishing Company, 1923.*

The Sloop Dropped Anchor, *oil on canvas, 30" x 21". From* The Crimson Cutlass *by Russell G. Carter,*
Penn Publishing Company, 1933. Courtesy Luther D. Reed.

Blackbeard in Smoke and Flame, *oil on canvas, 50" x 36". From* American Boy Magazine, *"Blackbeard the Buccaneer"*
by Ralph D. Paine, September, 1922. Collection Mr. and Mrs. Thomas Spackman.

Blackbeard Means Business, *charcoal and crayon on board, 15" x 8 1/2". From* American Boy Magazine, *"Blackbeard the Buccaneer"*
by Ralph D. Paine, May, 1922. Courtesy Sewell C. Biggs, Private Collection.

Pirate's Picnic Ashore, *oil on board, 108 1/2" x 66 3/8". Mural for Xanadu, home of Irénée duPont in Cardenas, Cuba, 1934. Picture now believed to be in Kremlin, Moscow, U.S.S.R.*

144

Frank Schoonover at work on his painting Pirate's Picnic Ashore.

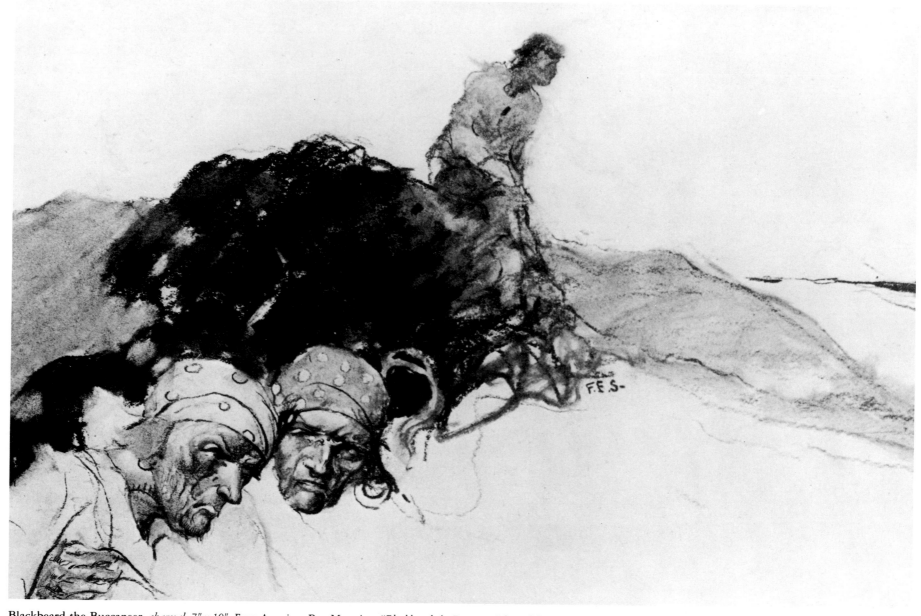

Blackbeard the Buccaneer, *charcoal, 7" x 10". From* American Boy Magazine, *"Blackbeard the Buccaneer" by Ralph D. Paine, June 1922. Courtesy Sewell C. Biggs Private Collection.*

The Christmas Boat, *oil on canvas, 36" x 30". From* American Boy Magazine, *"Blackbeard the Buccaneer" by Ralph D. Paine, July 1922.*

Pirates Approaching Prize Ship, *oil on board, 36" x 14". From* American Boy Magazine, *"Blackbeard the Buccaneer" by Ralph D. Paine, June 1922.*

Pirate with Spyglass, *oil on canvas, 33" x 22". From* The Treasure of St. Albans *written and illustrated by Frank Schoonover but never published, 1915.*

Privateers of '76, *oil on canvas, 34" x 30". From* Privateers of '76, *by Ralph D. Paine, jacket illustration, Penn Publishing Company, 1923. The Permanent Collection of the University of Delaware.*

How Strange It Seemed to Me a Boy, to Sit in the Prow, *oil on canvas, 36" x 27". From* American Boy Magazine, *"The White Blackfoot" by James Willard Schultz, March 1918.*

Sinking of the Yawl Boat, *oil on canvas, 18" x 12". From* A Jersey Boy in the Revolution *by Everett T. Tomlinson, Houghton Mifflin, 1899. Private collection. Photograph courtesy the Brandywine River Museum.*

ROBINSON CRUSOE
DANIEL DEFOE

Robinson Crusoe, *oil on canvas, 36" x 25". From* Robinson Crusoe *by Daniel Defoe, jacket illustration, Harper & Brothers, 1921.*

Rowena, *oil on canvas, 36" x 30". From* Ivanhoe *by Sir Walter Scott, Harper & Brothers, 1922. Collection St. Andrew's School.*

TALES FROM SHAKESPEARE

CHARLES AND MARY LAMB

Tales from Shakespeare, *oil on canvas, 36" x 28". From* Tales from Shakespeare
by Charles and Mary Lamb, jacket illustration, Harper & Brothers, 1918.

ROBIN HOOD

Robin Hood, *oil on canvas, 36" x 25". From* Robin Hood *by Roger L. Green, jacket illustration, Harper & Brothers, 1921.*

A Princess of Mars

EDGAR RICE BURROUGHS

A Princess of Mars, *oil on canvas, 34" x 25". From* A Princess of Mars *by Edgar Rice Burroughs, jacket illustration, A. C. McClurg Publishing Company, 1919.*

TOM BROWN'S SCHOOL DAYS

Tom Brown's School Days, *oil on canvas, 36" x 31".* From Tom Brown's School Days *by Thomas Hughes, jacket illustration, Harper & Brothers, 1921. Courtesy Permanent Collection of the Wilmington Trust Company, Wilmington, Delaware.*

Playing Craps, *charcoal on board, 16" x 20". From* Waifs of the Street *by Earnest C. Poole, S. S. McClure Company, 1903. Courtesy Sewell C. Biggs Private Collection.*

Heidi, *oil on canvas, 36" x 30". From* Heidi *by Johanna Spyri, jacket illustration, Harper & Brothers, 1924.*

GRIMM'S FAIRY TALES

Grimm's Fairy Tales, *oil on canvas, 36" x 28". From* Grimm's Fairy Tales *by The Brothers Grimm,
jacket and book cover, Harper & Brothers, 1921.*

Joan of Arc, *oil on canvas, 36" x 17". From Joan of Arc by Lucy Foster Madison, jacket illustration,*
Penn Publishing Company, 1918. Courtesy Tower Hill School, Wilmington, Delaware.

Joan of Arc Leading Troops across Bridge, *oil on canvas, 36" x 27". From* Joan of Arc *by Lucy Foster Madison, Penn Publishing Company, 1918. Courtesy Tower Hill School, Wilmington, Delaware.*

The Skipper Met Lafayette's Glance with Determination, *oil on canvas, 36" x 30". From* Lafayette
by Lucy Foster Madison, Penn Publishing Company, 1921. Courtesy Private Collection.

The Barque Flitmore, *oil on canvas, 36" x 30". From* Country Gentleman, *"The Barque Flitmore," 1937.*

Kidnapped, *oil on canvas, 36" x 28". From Kidnapped by Robert Louis Stevenson, jacket illustration, Harper & Brothers, 1921.*
Collection Chester Marron. Photograph courtesy the Brandywine River Museum.

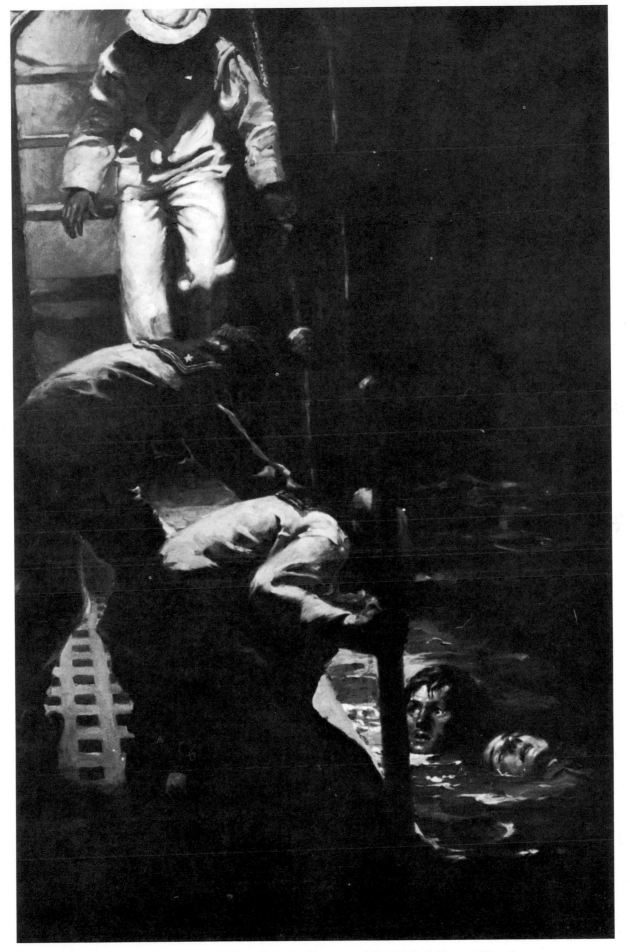

It Took Rathbone Eight Hours to Get Back to Helena, *oil on canvas, 34" x 22". From* Harper's Magazine,
"The Hero" by Margarita Spalding Gerry, February 1911. Courtesy Private Collection.

Pickett's Charge, *oil on canvas, 49" x 36". From* Progressive Farmer, *1938. Collection Mrs. Philip D. Laird, New Castle, Delaware.*

Pulling the Cannon, *oil on board, 18 1/2" x 12 1/4". From* McClure's Magazine, *"Colonial Frontiers at Louisburg" by Cyrus Townsend Bratty, September 1901. Courtesy Private Collection.*

You Are So Beautiful, *oil on board, 20" x 16". From* The Lane That Had No Turning *by Sir Gilbert Parker, Doubleday, Page & Company, 1902. Courtesy Private Collection.*

The General, *also called* **The Chase,** *charcoal on board, 28" x 24". From* McClure's Magazine, *"Andrew's Railroad Raid"*
by S. S. Parrot, September 1903. Courtesy Private Collection.

Lincoln, *oil on canvas, 36" x 30". From* Lincoln *by Lucy Foster Madison, Penn Publishing Company, 1928. Courtesy the Wilmington Savings Fund Society, Wilmington, Delaware.*

Lincoln-Douglas Debate, *oil on canvas, 30" x 26". From Lincoln by Lucy Foster Madison, Penn Publishing Company, 1928.*
Courtesy the Wilmington Savings Fund Society, Wilmington, Delaware.

Washington, the Surveyor, *oil on canvas, 36" x 30". From* Washington *by Lucy Foster Madison, Penn Publishing Company, 1925*

PAINTINGS

FRANK SCHOONOVER'S NUMEROUS LANDSCAPES AND EASEL PAINT-
INGS ARE NOTORIOUSLY BEAUTIFUL. HE ALSO WORKED EXTENSIVELY
ON MURALS AND RESTORATION OF HISTORICAL PORTRAITS, AL-
THOUGH PORTRAITURE WAS NOT HIS FIRST LOVE.

SCHOONOVER'S TONAL DRAWINGS AND PEN AND INK SKETCHES,
PARTICULARLY THOSE USED AS BOOK ILLUSTRATIONS, WERE UNSUR-
PASSED. SCHOONOVER ALSO TOOK AN INTEREST IN CARTOGRAPHY,
ILLUSTRATED HERE BY THE MAP, *THE MILLS ON THE BRANDYWINE,*
WHICH WAS USED FOR THE ENDPAPERS OF *DUPONT: THE AUTOBIOG-*
RAPHY OF AN AMERICAN ENTERPRISE, PRODUCED IN 1952.

HE DESIGNED BOOKPLATES FOR THE MAMIE EISENHOWER LIBRARY
AND FOR OTHER PROMINENT COLLECTIONS, INCLUDING THOSE OF
PIERRE DUPONT, IRÉNÉE DUPONT, ST. ANDREW'S SCHOOL IN MID-
DLETOWN, DELAWARE AND OTHERS.

Deer in Mist, *oil on canvas, 24" x 30", 1942. Courtesy of Mrs. A. B. C. Strange.*

At Last We Climbed the Steep Rim of the Magellan Range, *oil on canvas, 27" x 36".* From American Boy Magazine,
"The Questers of the Desert" by James Willard Stewart, June 1925. Courtesy Sewell C. Biggs Private Collection.

The Eel Weir, *oil on canvas, 30" x 40". Provident Life Insurance Company, Philadelphia, Pennsylvania, calendar, 1975, painted in 1949. Collection Mr. and Mrs. Thomas Spackman.*

The Valley and Mountains from Bensley Farm Road, *oil on canvas, 32" x 28", 1944.*

The Bensley Farm, *oil on canvas, 28" x 32", 1945.*

Bend of Big Bushkill at Cake Out, *oil on canvas, 28" x 32", 1944.*

John Le Bar's House, *oil on canvas, 36" x 40", 1946. Courtesy Hotel DuPont, Wilmington, Delaware.*

Roadway above Village of Bushkill, Pa., *oil on canvas, 30" x 44", 1948. Collection Immanuel Church, Wilmington, Delaware.*

Du Pont Powder Mills on the Brandywine, *oil on canvas, 42" x 47". Plate Design used by The Brandywine Valley Association, 1973, painted in 1958. Private Collection. Photograph courtesy the Brandywine River Museum.*

The Lost Battalion, *oil on canvas, 30" x 50". From* The Ladies' Home Journal, *February 1919. Courtesy the Delaware National Guard, Wilmington, Delaware.*

In Flanders Fields, *oil on canvas, 30" x 50". From* The Ladies' Home Journal, *May 1919.*

Home From the War, *oil on canvas, 36" x 30". From* Country Gentleman, *"The Singing River" by Zane Grey, September 1929.*

Sergeant James P. Connor, *oil on canvas, 30" x 25", 1945. Courtesy Division of Historical and Cultural Affairs, Department of State, Dover, Delaware.*

(Above and right) Sketches for Capture of the Galleon, *see overleaf.*

190

Capture of the Galleon, *oil on canvas,
108 1/2" x 66 3/4". Mural decoration
for Xanadu, home of Irénée DuPont
in Cardenas, Cuba, 1934. Picture now
belived to be in Kremlin, Moscow, Russia.*

As a Witch, *oil on board, 20" x 16", 1901. Courtesy Private Collection.*

Cleaning up Cotton Fields, *oil on canvas, 30" x 36". From* Country Gentleman, *"Bread and Stones" by Jack Bethea, September 1927. Collection Mrs. Harry W. Lynch.*

Female Portrait, *oil on canvas, 24" x 20", 1899. Courtesy Sewell C. Biggs, Private Collection.*

Miracle Mary on the Way to Sing Sing, *oil on canvas, 18" x 24". From* American Boy Magazine, *"Miracle Mary" by John A. Moroso, December 1913. Courtesy Private Collection.*

Santa Claus in Balloon, *oil on canvas, 30" x 26". From* Popular Magazine *cover illustration, December 7, 1928. Courtesy The Wooden Shoe Collection, Chadds Ford, Pa.*

Original Immanuel Church, *Wilmington, Delaware, stained-glass window designed by Frank Schoonover in 1942.*

CHRONOLOGY
Frank E. Schoonover, 1877–1972

1877   19 August, Frank Earle Schoonover born, Oxford, New Jersey. Son of Colonel John and Elizabeth La Barre Schoonover

1891   Graduated with second High Honors from the Model School, Trenton, New Jersey. Gave Salutatory Address

1896   Entered Art School, Drexel Institute, Philadelphia, Pennsylvania

1897   Admitted to Howard Pyle's composition class at Drexel

1898   Attended Howard Pyle's summer art school at Chadds Ford, Pennsylvania. First painting sold, a landscape, from the exhibition of work by Mr. Pyle's students at Turner's Mill

1899   Attended Mr. Pyle's summer art school at Chadds Ford for the second summer. Both years he was an honor scholarship student

1899   7 August, started work on drawing #1, "Nearer and Nearer They Approached," one of four drawings for *A Jersey Boy in the Revolution* by Evert E. Tomlinson, published by Houghton Mifflin and Company

1899   1 September, moved into his first studio at 11 East 8th Street, Wilmington, Delaware

1900   Moved his studio to 1305 Franklin Street, Wilmington, where he and Stanley M. Arthurs lived with Howard Pyle

1903   November, set out on expedition which was to take him over 1,200 miles by dogsled and snowshoe in the Hudson Bay and James Bay areas of Quebec and Ontario, Canada

1905   11 March, became member of the society of Illustrators, Inc., in New York City

1905   April, "The Edge of Wilderness," first story written and illustrated by F. E. Schoonover, published by *Scribner's Magazine*

1906   Elected to membership in the Franklin Inn Club, Philadelphia, Pennsylvania

1906   9 January to 1 February, made trip to Jamaica with Howard Pyle and Stanley M. Arthurs.

1906   8 March, moved to his own studio at 1616 Rodney Street, Wilmington, Delaware, where he worked for the remainder of his career

1906   Elected Hereditary Companion of the Loyal Legion of the United States: insignia 14959, Commandery of the State of Pennsylvania

1907	Toured Europe in the company of Richard Sellers of Wilmington, Delaware, studying the works of the great masters and visiting museums and churches, most of all in Italy
1908	Elected to membership in The Players in New York City, where he stayed often on visits to publishers and friends
1909	Became member of the Racquet Club, Philadelphia, Pennsylvania
1910	Assisted Howard Pyle to produce a large (9′ x 36′) mural for the Hudson County Courthouse, Jersey City, New Jersey
1911	18 January, married Martha Culbertson of Philadelphia, Pennsylvania
1911	Spring and summer, made his second expedition to Canada, this time by canoe and portage in the northern and western Province of Ontario
1911	December, appearance in *Harper's Magazine* of short story written and illustrated by Schoonover, "The Haunts of Jean Lafitte." His wife did the background research
1912 to 1918	A period of intensive writing and illustrating for magazines and books
1912	27 November, Incorporated the Wilmington Society of the Fine Arts of which he was a lifetime director and chairman of many exhibitions. Chairman of fund-raising committee to procure Howard Pyle Collection
1912	Founding and life member of the Quill and Grill Society of Wilmington, Delaware
1914	1 January, became member of the Fellowship of the Philadelphia Academy of the Fine Arts
1914	5 January, only son, Cortlandt, born
1914	Acquired his first summer studio in Hemingway's Mill in Bushkill, Pennsylvania. Later he built a larger summer studio on his own property, where he worked summers
1918	8 July, only daughter, Elizabeth Louise, born
1919	Painted series of World War I pictures for the *Ladies' Home Journal*. Most of these are now in the Department of Defense, Washington, D. C.
1920 to 1930	Illustrated many classics and children's books, among them *Robinson Crusoe, Kidnapped, Heidi, Gulliver's Travels, Swiss Family Robinson,* and *Grimm's Fairy Tales*. Also during this period illustrated such books as *Lincoln, Lafayette, Roland the Warrior, Joan of Arc,* and many others—over 200 throughout his career
1924	President and lifetime member of the Church Club of Delaware
1925	Organized the Wilmington Sketch Club with Gayle Hoskins, a fellow Howard Pyle student. The Club still flourishes and is housed in Mr. Pyle's Franklin Street studio
1930	Designed first of a series of 16 stained-glass windows for Immanuel Episcopal Church, Wilmington, Delaware
1931	Organized School of Illustration for the John Herron Art Institute of Indianapolis, Indiana, and lectured there for a time, writing the text material and using his own paintings for teaching illustration
1935	President and lifetime member of the Lincoln Club of Delaware; designed the emblem of the club

1937   Beginning of period of landscape painting which continued for the rest of his active career. His favorite locales were the upper Delaware River Valley and the Brandywine River Valley

1942   Started his own art school in Wilmington, Delaware which he continued until shortly before suffering a stroke in 1968

1959   12 January, completed 41 years' service as Warden of Immanuel Episcopal Church, Wilmington, Delaware. For 40 of these years, he was Senior Warden, and for the balance of his life, Senior Warden Emeritus

1962   Acclaimed by Delaware Press as "Dean of Delaware Artists," a title he held for the rest of his life

1962   5 October, one-man Retrospective Exhibition at the Wilmington Society of the Fine Arts (now the Delaware Art Museum)

1963   16 September, Honorary Master of Arts degree conferred by the University of Delaware, Newark, Delaware

1968   1 December, suffered first of a series of strokes which left his left side paralyzed and effectively terminated his artistic career.

1970   Recipient Edgar Rice Burroughs Bibliophile's National Award

1972   1 September, died at the age of 95, Wilmington, Delaware. Buried in Old St. Anne's Cemetery, Middletown, Delaware

1974   3 October, posthumous publication of *The Edge of the Wilderness: A Portrait of the Canadian North,* by Frank E. Schoonover, edited by Cortlandt Schoonover, published by Methuen Publications, Toronto, Ontario, Canada.

INDEX